Poetry and Other Inspired Ideas

My transformational journey to healing

Poetry and Other Inspired Ideas

My transformational journey to healing

RHONDA WILLIAMS

Copyright © 2021 by RHONDA WILLIAMS.

All rights reserved. No part of this book may be reproduced in any form or by any electronic or mechanical means, including information storage and retrieval systems, without permission in writing from the publisher, except by reviewers, who may quote brief passages in a review.

ISBN: 978-1-956515-29-9 (Paperback Edition)
ISBN: 978-1-956515-30-5 (Hardcover Edition)
ISBN: 978-1-956515-28-2 (E-book Edition)

Book Ordering Information

Phone Number: 315 288-7939 ext. 1000 or 347-901-4920
Email: info@globalsummithouse.com
Global Summit House
www.globalsummithouse.com

Printed in the United States of America

Dedication

To my parents, the late Ronald and Gloria Williams, whom I now realize did the best they could to give me the best life. Also, to my inner child, as I salute the Christ in her that lay dormant for so long until she was strong enough to emerge—to be heard continuously and clearly and spearhead the healing process of my soul.

Contents

Foreword II
Preface III
Acknowledgments IV
Introduction VII
My Proetry XV

Part 1

    The Evolution Process 17
    First Process 19
    So Sorry I Didn't Know 20
    I Need Peace From the Pain 21
    Why Do I Keep Falling in the Well? 22
    Invisible in Your Own Light 23
    Wake Up the Warrior Within 24
    Second Process 25
    Mirror, Mirror 26
    Shine a Spotlight on My Life 27
    In Step with Spirit 28
    Letting Go 29
    Reasons for the Seasons 30
    Third Process 31
    Soul Food Supplement 32
    Defeating the Enemy 33
    Put Your Armor On 34
    Release Another Layer to the Light 35
    Pit Stop to Transformation Nation 36

Fourth Process 37
Self-Love Is the Key 38
I Am the Light that I Seek 39
Message to My Creator 40
Path to Peace 41
Celebrate 42

Part II
Visualized Healing Meditations 44
Releasing 45
New Moon 47
Your Higher Self 49
Candles In The Mirror 51

Part III
Affirmations 54
I Know 55
I Believe 57
I Am 59
Prosperity Affirmations 61
Letter to Self-Forgiveness 63
Letter to Forgiveness 65

Glossary
Recommended Reading

Foreword

Rhonda Williams' book, *Poetry and Other Inspired Ideas: My transformational journey to healing*, is a heartfelt chronicle of her path to God/Self Realization. It is a path we are all called to walk, and Rhonda's book gives us delicious spiritual food for our journey.

Over the last several years, I've had the privilege of witnessing Rhonda evolve and develop into an amazing channel for the Holy Spirit of God and the Archangelic Realms. Like Rhonda herself, the book is full of warmth, humor, grace, love and most importantly truth.

The story is told through beautiful inspired poetry and soulful prose that shares her journey. As I read the poems, I felt the Energy of God calling me into prayer and communion. The book also offers us guided meditations, affirmations and visualizations for the journey.

As we read Rhonda's journey, we understand it is our journey. There is only one journey we all share. Thank you, God!

I invite you to open your heart and soul and enjoy this wonderful book!

Reverend Daniel Neusom

Author of *On Earth As It Is In Heaven* and *You Are Here On The Earth To Enjoy Everything*

Cofounder and Spiritual Director of the Sacred Light Fellowship, NY, NY

Preface

Growth comes about as a result of what you are willing to learn. As I began sharing my experiences through these writings, sometimes I found it hard to recognize myself in my own words. I now believe that what Spirit said to me was true. My earth's work is to be able to share my God-given talents with the world in order to spread peace, joy, love and happiness using arts and entertainment.

I feel privileged to recommend this book to anyone seeking spiritual development, personal growth, healing and transformation. My hope is that this book may assist and inspire each reader along their own journey to awareness.

Acknowledgments

I would like to first acknowledge, in spiritual order, my board of directors: the Creator of the Universe, Mother Mary, our elder brother Jesus, the Archangels Michael, Raphael, Gabriel and Uriel, and all of my angels and spirit guides.

To Iyanla Vanzant for her writings and teachings which helped kick-start interest in my spiritual development.

To my beloved television ministers: Joel Osteen (a.k.a. Cousin Joel),

T.D. Jakes (a.k.a. Brother Jakes) and Joyce Meyer (a.k.a. Auntie Joyce) for their positive and humorous talks about their journeys and coming into their authentic selves.

To Dr. Wayne W. Dyer who inspired me to move forward as I studied his words of wisdom in special programs aired on PBS stations.

To Oprah Winfrey for all of her years of teaching her truths through my television set, especially Super Soul Sundays.

In the late 2000's when I attended an Easter Sunday service at a spiritual center in New York City known as Sacred Light Fellowship(*www.sacredlightfellowship.org*), of which I am now an active member. A beloved thanks to the founders of this special place: Rev. Lyn Skreczko Van Riper, Revs. George and Catherine Brooks and Rev. Daniel Neusom (also a published author).

Rev. Daniel Neusom has become my teacher, mentor and friend. Because of his compassion, dedication and guidance in our church and congregation, I was able to embrace my experiences and become a perpetual student of my life. From this place of awareness, I was able to embrace the possibilities of discovering my true God self.

I must include all members of the congregation, past and present, that continue to support and uplift me to my fullest potential and beyond: Rev. Barbara Robinson, Rev. Ethel Walker, Rev. Frank Craven, Rev. Julie Berndt, Rev. Andrew Harriott, Minister of Music Nathlyn Flowers, Frances A. Smokowski, Revalyn Gold, Thomas Horray and Michele Danels.

Special thanks to my sister from another mister, Adina Settles, a longtime friend and confidante who put me on my path to prayer by giving me *The Prayer of Jabez* by Bruce Wilkinson. Special thanks to Lynn Allison (a.k.a. Inspiration), "a true humanitarian by divine design" and my spiritual sidekick for the love, concern and willingness to keep me focused on my goals. Special thanks to Claudia Brown who was my go-to person for feedback on this book. Special thanks to Dr. Ali Yasin and the family of the Billionaire Mastermind Forum (***www.billionairemastermindforum.com***).

Thanks to my life coach, Darvi Mack (www.darvimack.com). Because of her tough love, intelligence, total commitment and encouragement to move forward fearlessly, I was propelled to the path of my true purpose and for this I will be eternally grateful.

Thanks to my Reiki Masters, Randi Ditman-Ibrahim and Carmen Lariño, for teaching me to become a Reiki practitioner at the Center for Living Light in New York. Thanks to my fellow practitioner and author, Peter Bruce Reiter. In addition, thanks to my fellow practitioner and friend Elizabeth O. Tinuoye for her continued, steadfast support throughout the entire growth process of my book and journey.

To Andrew Morrison for his powerful and generous teleseminar "How to Write a Best Seller in 30 Days."

To Maya Angelou, one of my she-roes and a literary lady of our lineage.

I must never forget my stepmother, Carolyn Anthony Williams, and her many gifts. Carolyn's unconditional love for all of her family was unwavering as well as her generosity, kindness, patience and understanding.

I thank God for Carolyn and her contribution to my spiritual growth and development. We are blessed to continue our connection after her transition and for this I will be eternally grateful.

Ultimately, I will forever be grateful to Dianne Crawley (a.k.a. "Cuz") from my extended family for all of her compassion, effort, time and support in every way with the re-edit of this project. I thank you for being in my life for so many years!

I love you all!

Introduction

I had been a functioning drug and alcohol user, with cigarettes on the side, for decades. My drugs of choice were marijuana and cocaine. My alcohol of choice was rum, with beer and wine as chasers (always an overachiever!). They were my true crew.

During this time, I worked two jobs, traveled and took care of my responsibilities, and I never went without anything I needed. My family was aware of my issues. They were, of course, disappointed. But I was an adult making my own choices about how to live my life. Being their first child and only daughter, *you can imagine how proud my parents were of me.*

I was very selfish and self-centered and did only what pleased me. Using drugs and drinking alcohol was my pleasure and none of their business. They accepted and loved me as much as they could and as much as I would allow them.

My mother and I were good girlfriends and enjoyed doing girlfriend things together, such as shopping, dining out, going to movies, plays, museums and traveling. There were regular attempts to outwit each other and always lots of laughter. We had our typical mother-daughter issues, but for the most part, we were solid.

In 1996, three months after she retired, my mother's sudden death of natural causes was devastating! *My best bud was gone without any warning*. I went through the motions dealing with daily routines. Thankfully, she had taken care of all the details of her going-home celebration, right down to the burial attire, service, plot and limos. No fuss, no muss!

I looked to the brighter side, seeing it as another excuse to hang out with the "true crew", my girls—cocaine, rum and marijuana (a.k.a.

Coco, Rummy and Mary J) and cigarettes on the side. *So glad you ladies are still with me! We have been friends for so long, and I need you in my life now more than ever!*

Fast forward to January 2004. After a two-week battle with bronchitis, nicotine (a.k.a. Nicky) was voted off the island. The other ladies were laying low because the prescription drugs for bronchitis took priority. In return, I was able to breathe properly and I saved a lot of money. I also lost the desire for Nicky. *Bye, buddy!* I strongly believe the Holy Spirit removed the desire from my conscious and subconscious mind. However, the remainder of my true crew returned soon after I started feeling like my old self again.

In November 2007, for some reason I started losing the desire for Coco! What was happening? This was my favorite party time of year and this made no sense to me. I was able to "just say no" for the first time in over three decades! Another one voted off the island, but how and why now? My girl Mary J was a trooper. She joined the crew after Nicky and Rummy and was hanging on. I was grateful because I believed that she still served a purpose.

By the mid-2000s, my dad had become my best friend. It was a few years after my mother passed away and after his divorce from his second wife. Two swinging singles were we! We did best friend things together—movies, Coney Island, cookouts, dining out. But mostly we loved cooking and hanging out on his terrace and listening to his extensive collection of jazz that he loved so dearly while eating, drinking and cracking jokes. We had lots of laughter and weekend sleepovers. Life was great! I had the relationship with my dad I longed for as a child. This was part of the divine plan and I was ever so grateful.

In January 2007, I was grieving the loss of grandpa, my father's dad. Daddy and grandpa had a unhappy relationship which was lifelong. Years of unresolved tension between them left all three of us with many unresolved issues.

That's when my relationship with Daddy took a wrong turn. Every week I went to Pathmark for his groceries. One day he started fussing that I bought the wrong things. My false ego took over and I released a verbal fury over the phone that had been suppressed for years. My five minute rant at my best friend released a truckload of feelings. I hung up the phone abruptly and I felt relieved because I finally said what I had been holding in for so long. However, the relief was short lived because it was followed by guilt, shame, disgust, emptiness and disrespect for my dad and myself. I knew our relationship would change. What had I done to the *us* that we had developed? After working so hard to get to this place of trust and respect, in minutes, I singlehandedly destroyed everything I wanted and needed since childhood.

For months, we had no contact. Our relationship now mirrored the relationship Daddy had with his father. We were both too stubborn and too proud to reach out to each other, so we chose silence instead of forgiveness. I did not know it at the time, but we both needed healing separately. I chose to turn my attention to becoming more spiritual and explored what my church had to offer. My dad chose his way.

I was still hanging on to Mary J, the last of the true crew, and occasionally a little Rummy on the side because I needed to fill yet another void in my life. The Sacred Light Fellowship served me well as a sanctuary and as an opening that led to learning new and positive teachings of healing and transformation, *whatever that was!* It just felt right.

Months went by as I settled into my new mind-set and consciousness, but I had not heard from my dad. Learning to be more spiritual and in touch with my higher self, I decided to bite the bullet and reach out to him. Dad was hesitant but receptive, and we started over as if nothing had happened. We were both grateful, but never spoke about it because we both knew it would be too painful and it served no purpose to relive that experience. I am so glad we did. Our first play date was on Good Friday, 2009. How cool was that? I had my best friend back! Thank you, God!

My dad was diagnosed with lymphoma in July 2009. For years, he had been monitored for prostate cancer, so this was a total shock! After only a few treatments of chemotherapy, he became unable to release his bowels and was in so much pain he decided to go to the emergency room. In the ER, a low immune system is like being naked in a snow storm in Alaska. He never had a chance. He called and left a message on my voicemail. I rushed to the hospital and found him resting and being treated. We talked for a while, then he wanted to get some rest. He sent me to his home to get some personal things he needed, and I planned to come back in the morning. When I returned the next day later than he expected, he was annoyed because of my lateness. Also, I had forgotten to bring his newspaper. He was not happy and let me know it! I became frustrated and angry with him and chose to stay for only a short time. Little did I know it would be the last time we would speak. Also, it would be the last time I would hang out with Mary J. She was the last one standing for a long time. But I knew that I could not, and would not, be able to go to the hospital and subsequently the hospice high! The doctors, nurses and staff would see and would know. I did not want to disrespect my dad. So, on September 20, 2009, I decided Mary J no longer served a purpose and cold turkey was the answer. Thank you, God!

My dad transitioned in late November 2009. He had rested in one of the best hospice facilities in the country. I was so grateful we had been brought back together before the end. All a part of His divine plan!

Another blessing would be my stepmother, Carolyn Anthony Williams. In her, I was fortunate to find more of a second mom than a stepmom (no Cinderella story here). With her unique style of mothering and nurturing, she was able to make our extended families work effortlessly, even including my birth mother, Gloria. We had a special mother-daughter relationship, even after their divorce. Carolyn was instrumental in assisting me before and after my dad's transition.

Carolyn's religious and spiritual beliefs also guided me gently through some of the darkness that followed my dad's death. Her special gift to me, that I still treasure, is the big beautiful Joyce Meyer Bible, for which she "saved her pennies" to order and deliver to me. We were both proud because now we each had one and we both loved Joyce Meyer. The Book of Psalms became my favorite "go to" reference. I believe that my "proetry" reflects some of the faith and flow of The Psalms, a much needed tool in these trying times!

Another part of my path was Sacred Light Fellowship (SLF), and it was a great comfort through my mourning period. In the spring of 2010, I went to my first retreat ever with SLF. It was a wonderful day trip to an upstate New York venue that was perfect for our congregation. The day was sunny, warm and breezy. The grounds overlooked the Hudson River and we could see New Jersey. All the boats and activities on the water were surreal. The retreat included worship, seminars, dining, meditation, prayer, Reiki healing and some networking as well.

During some down time, people chose to gather in small groups and share their experiences. I chose to sit under a tree and write in my journal as I gazed out onto the river and enjoyed my toes. This felt like home and I was at peace.

Toward the end of the day, people were exchanging business cards. One of my spiritual sisters gave me contact information for a daily teleconference with people who shared their success stories and uplifted others interested in improving their lives through mind, body and spirit. Collectively, we connected and inspired one another with affirmations. Guest speakers shared their success stories and products with participants to enhance the experience. I never heard of people so dedicated, positively focused and open to supporting others on their journeys to fulfill their purpose. Some members were already successful entrepreneurs, authors, home-based businesses and network marketing; each bringing something special to the table. *Imagine being able to dial in and connect with a whole new world that I never knew existed.* I had found a comfortable new home.

Starting a home-based business is hard enough when you have some knowledge of what you are doing. But when you do not know and you do not follow your supervisor's instructions, this is a recipe for failure. Trying to reinvent the wheel? Why? "Never underestimate the ruthlessness of the ego," says Ilyana Vanzant. And it was not pretty!

After about a year of mismanaging my finances through unhealthy spending, traveling to conferences, shopping, hotels, meals, business cards and other marketing ideas, I finally maxed out my credit cards and was in debt. I made almost no profit. Thank God for my full-time job!

I felt depressed, disgusted, disgraced, ashamed and guilty. I could no longer listen to my favorite teleconferences, seminars or workshops. I did not feel worthy, especially after my cell phone was disconnected. I decided not to attend any company meetings or gatherings. I could not even look at my Facebook page and see all the people with whom I had networked. We had so much fun and so much in common only a short time ago. Now they were moving on without me!

My spirit was broken. I stopped going to church. I stopped being supportive to anyone, especially myself. I resented everyone and everything. This went on for months!

I decided to use prayer for comfort. I read prayers written by others, some Bible verses and listened to TV preachers. A lot of emotional release came after these sessions. It took a long time before I started to feel a little better each day. I could not explain it and didn't want to. I was just glad to be in a better place. I was starving for peace in my spirit and soul. I was too proud to ask for help and didn't know how. I had always chosen to suffer in silence, but this time I realized I had another choice. God was always there waiting for me to be open to His light.

After many sessions of emotional release, prayer and meditation, my poems started to surface. I would get up in the middle of the day or night and write down the words I received in my mind that rhymed. *OMG! What was happening? I wasn't sure, but it felt good. Keep them coming.* And they did!

The word "proetry" is a fusion of prayer and poetry, a powerful tool for my healing and transformation.

My Proetry

My proetry is of me, through me and for me,

but not the me I claim to be.

It flows naturally at any given time,

but never having the feeling of being mine.

Spirit touches me and I begin to write.

There seems to be no end

in sight. What a gift and I am so blessed.

Don't try to figure it out, just give it my best

and never mind about the rest.

All is well!

Part 1

The Evolution Process

First Process
Awakening {More storms = more growth}

Second Process
Accepting {My best friend is right within}

Third Process
Adhering {Pace yourself to embrace yourself}

Fourth Process
Allowing {All avenues can lead to peace}

Spirituality is the essence of my evolutionary process.
As I evolve, my conscious and subconscious change.
This fuels my thirst for personal growth and
comes in stages that create my proetry.

First Process

Awakening {More storms = more growth}
Praise God through the *pain*…the *storms*…and the *rain*

So Sorry I Didn't Know

So sorry I didn't know
how far away from You I had to go.

To realize all that I already
had, instead always
choosing to be sad.

Didn't know to be thankful, grateful or even
aware that no matter what I did, You would
always care.

Only complaining about what was
not. Year after year, didn't know
how to stop.

I needed to have faith in my faith to pull myself along,
holding on tight to Your love to keep me strong.

So now I know without
a doubt, and it is never too
late to find You out.

I Need Peace From the Pain

Every step I take coming closer to victory,
there is no peace from the pain.
I cannot see a break for me.
I need peace from the pain.
Struggle too long, everything still going wrong.
Give me peace from the pain.
I continue to follow the words You show.
Still no peace from the pain.
Around the mountain and down below,
where is the peace from the pain?
Grateful! Thankful! Hopeful!
Send me peace from the pain.
Help me now Lord, I am not that tough.
I am ready for the peace from the pain.
I must confess, I will pass this test,
then look back and know it was not all in vain.

Why Do I Keep Falling in the Well?

It is still dark and lonely.
Nothing has changed since I was here last.
I tripped and fell yet again off my path.

My bumpy road with its twists and turns
seems the only way I have chosen to learn.

Familiar surroundings damp, dark and bleak.
The part of me that feels undeserving wants to speak,
but it is still muffled by pain and I am afraid to take the leap.

The leap into the light because there waits my fate.
I know this cycle needs to break.

I try to continue my prayers and ask for grace
to take me and keep me from this awful place.

Why do I keep falling in the well?
It's all a part of the journey and only time will tell.

Invisible in Your Own Light

Many around you may shout your praise,

then suddenly there is silence for days and days.

Days turn into weeks and weeks turn into months.

It only happens when you stand out front.

In front of the crowd, you stand proud,

forgetting that there is always a cloud.

Clouds form storms that wreak havoc in your life.

Be ready for the stress and strife.

Use this time to remember the Truth

that the Holy Spirit is always in hot pursuit.

Try to continue your healing and move forward with grace.

Without God's love, the world is a lonely place.

Breathe in deeply and hold on to your dreams.

Exhale and release your fears, life is not always what it seems.

Acknowledge you accomplishments

and support your own rights.

If left undone, you will become invisible in your own light.

Wake Up the Warrior Within

The sleep of forgetfulness showed up and stayed,
never have I been so dismayed.

It continued to block the light of Your love,
rejecting rays of hope from above.

All my life I've known the strength You gave.
When I looked for it and needed it, it was hiding in a cave.

The cave of my soul snuggled safe as can be,
waiting patiently for Your light to set it free.

Forgot who I was!
Forgot who to be!
Forgot why I came here and what You promised me.

Holy Spirit seeks me and I open one eye.
Fear leaves me as I begin to cry.

It is the time to shine and the honor is all mine,
to wake up the warrior within
announcing my rebirth and reconnection.

Second Process

Accepting {My best friend is right within}

Don't just *go* through it, *grow* through it.

Mirror, Mirror

I will always love you no matter what you say or do.

We need each other more now than ever.
There is no time to be cute or clever.

The truth is here and staring us right in the face.
It is the same yesterday, today and always,
never to be erased.

Forgiving ourselves is a great start,
knowing that nothing can tear us apart.

Faith is constant, feels safe and warm,
and surrendering will do us no harm.

Accept the love and light trying to break through,
awaiting the awareness of that magnificent you.

Our mirrored reflection helps us find our voice
and reminds us that we always have a choice.

To love each other as lifelong friends
because learning and teaching never ends.

Shine a Spotlight on My Life

Shine a spotlight on my life.

Show me all the stress and strife

so it can continue to remind me how

I am too close to give up now.

Too much has been done.

Too many battles have been won.

Proving that You still remain supreme

no matter how hard things may seem.

Thanks for the good times, the storms and the pain.

There were times I thought I would go insane.

My attitude of gratitude serves me proud,

especially when I cry out loud!

You are my Rock!

Never ever, ever stop!

In Step with Spirit

Salute yourself every day and on every level.

Embrace your gentleness and self-control.

Don't dance with the devil.

Never hold back thankful tears.

They are for your emotional release,

put in place to help you find peace.

Patience, love and joy always lie at your feet.

Use your passions and desires to help feel complete,

not envy or deceit.

Learn to know your own worth,

then celebrate your power

and count your blessings every hour.

Breakdowns bring breakthroughs.

Breakthroughs bring breakaways.

Breakaways can save the day

and will keep you in step with Spirit all the way.

Letting Go

Mindfully I no longer live in the land of lack.

I'm fighting every day not to look back.

The old ways of wisdom continue to clash.

I must leave my stinkin' thinkin' in the past

to open doors for future bliss

and allow the happiness in my life to exist.

Through the door of my heart enters love, light and truth.

My spirit smiles and shows all the proof.

The positive party begins right on time.

All souls are aligned with The Divine.

The splendor of Holy Spirit continues to show.

We have no reason not to let go.

Hold tight to your faith because it must be fed.

Remember to say your prayers before going to bed.

Pray for the world,

knowing that we are all connected

and our lives will never be what we expected.

Reasons for the Seasons

Change is growth and with growth comes pain.

Nothing can ever remain the same.

Our minds, bodies and spirits evolve

without our permission, we are not even involved.

We all play a role, everything in its place,

all beings share and occupy this space.

This cycle will continue long after we are gone.

Since we are living in the here and now, we have to be strong.

Have faith and know it is all part of The Divine Plan.

Decide now to take a stand,

a stand to bring your best game.

I guarantee you your life will change.

Let go and let God, not always easy to do.

But in our heart of hearts, we know it is true.

These are the reasons for the seasons.

Third Process

Adhering {Pace yourself to enjoy yourself}

Embrace and believe as you *explore* your truth.

Soul Food Supplement

Chew on the Word of God for your daily bread.

Take time to get to know Him and you will never be misled.

Scriptures can be soulful vitamins,

they may help to light the way.

Trust in Him and His Glory and learn something new everyday.

Set your table with patience, perseverance

and placemats woven of fine thread.

Always say a prayer for those not yet fed.

Accept this appetizer as my gift to you,

there are individual servings waiting too.

Raise a cup to salute your spirit that needs to be the boss. Enjoy this creature of habit and proceed to the next course.

Defeating the Enemy

Taking baby steps in grown-up shoes,

making sure the enemy will always lose.

Proving yourself to yourself leaves nothing to doubt

and makes it easier to keep the enemy out.

Mistakes make God love you more.

There are no challenges you cannot endure.

Perfect performances for Him are not needed.

Remember the enemy can always be defeated.

No longer fear your own magnificence,

just celebrate and embrace its significance.

Put Your Armor On

Peace is a position of power.

Don't dismiss it, own it every hour.

Put your armor on and stand strong in your splendor.

To God, and not the enemy, you must surrender.

Use your own:

Crown of Confidence

Cloak of Clarity

Helmet of Hope

Ring of Righteousness

Shield of Faith

Sword of Salvation

Sandals of Peace

These tools will help your faith increase.

Not writing this just for me,

the whole world needs to see.

Continue to put your armor on to live free and stay free!

Release Another Layer to the Light

Bow down before God and let go, don't fight.

Faith is the refuge through long, lonely nights.

Be still and know that freedom is near,
it comes closer with every tear.

Angels and guides await our call
because alone we cannot do it all.

Our hearts are heavy, pain is real
and it helps to remember that we are a big deal.

With open arms I plead my case
to send love into this space.

Brother Jesus walks with me to my holy place
and we are proudly escorted by Mother Grace.

So let's make things right.
It's time to release another layer to the light.

Pit Stop to Transformation Nation

All aboard, get your tickets! It's a local not an express.
If you miss this one, you can just take the next.

Get a window seat to see left and right.
The visions of your life can be quite a sight.

To your left, Lack Boulevard in Failure Falls
on the corner of Pain Parkway and Struggle Road.
Ah! We can see it all.
Coming up next, Anger Avenue across

from Frustration Junction.
What is your function?

To your right, Abundant Boulevard and Prosperity Place
on the corner of Success Street.
See Mount Freedom across from Good Rich Road.

Look, there is Joyful Junction.
Now that's my function!

Are you visiting, renting or just passing through?
It's all up to you.
Decide today on your way to Peaceville, USA.

Fourth Process

Allowing {All avenues can lead to peace}

Freedom is a *friend* to the fearless.

Self-Love Is the Key

I address my weakness to conquer my fear.
I make it clear to stand right here in my greatness.

Focus on my dreams no matter how extreme,
these unlimited possibilities God has foreseen.

I open my heart and breathe in Your Light
through each chakra, relax no need to fight.

I bathe in the truth of my soul's desire
knowing Mother Grace and Her love never expires.

Let my spirit soar, it cries to be free.

Loving myself is the only key!

I Am the Light that I Seek

Always looking outward for the love and peace I need,
forgetting that to my Mother/Father God, I am the seed.
The seed that has been so carefully planted by my entire being
and one of my assignments is to nurture it by seeing.
Seeing the beauty, love and kindness
in everyone I meet and greet
helps water my soul so I may feel complete.
Seeing and sharing my blessings every day,
sometimes meeting my gratitude half way.

I am the light that I seek!

By praising my triumphs and trials,
I continue to support my inner child.
Still I move forward with fear and doubt
looking for someone else to work it all out.
I must always look to the light within
because there it waits for the reconnection.
And I ask Spirit to let that be my daily intention.
So the last thing that I must mention –

I am the light that I seek!

Message to My Creator

Today as I dine on divine daily bread
I believe I am fully fed.

You guide me just where I need to be
so I can open my eyes and clearly see
this awesome life that gives me praise,
including unlimited opportunities every day.

I am listening louder now. Faith is stronger.
Can't figure it out, will not try any longer.

Surrendering helps me to breathe in Your loving light,
expanding my visions that explode during the night.
I handle life's challenges with taste and grace
to keep a happy smile upon my face.

Enjoy the journey with no worries or regrets.
Sit back and let You do the rest.

Path to Peace

Peace for me is walking in my truth,
never having to appear aloof.

My feet are placed firmly on the ground.
I will not stumble when I try to turn around.

Turn around to address new challenges through lessons learned.
My fears are no longer my concern.

My voice is stronger, no longer a whisper.
It echoes loudly in my soul as a twin sister.

Abandoned but not forgotten,
in my mind I have survived my past.
Saluting my entire being as it arrives home at last.

Celebrate

As I wallow in my wonderfulness,
I see visions of things not yet addressed.

Treating myself like a guest in my own life
allows me to release all darkness to the light.

Celebrate your self-love all day long.
It helps to keep you strong.
Strong in knowing you are the best you can be,
then every day you can grow naturally.

As a watered seedling, you rise to the sky,
never looking back or asking why.

Celebrate your richness as you explore your power.
You will be amazed by your beauty every hour.

Celebrate the dissolving of our she-gos and he-gos
by inviting Holy Spirit's love energy to flow.

Into our minds, bodies and souls to unite
and celebrate our oneness as a worldwide beacon of light.

And so it is!

Part II

Visualized Healing Meditations

Visualized healing meditations are often helpful when offering meditation to groups at churches, Reiki circles, spiritual seminars and workshops. In some cases during these experiences, additional healing and transformation are accepted and received.

Releasing

Close your eyes and sit back in your chair with your feet firmly on the floor. As you begin to relax, take three deep breaths and exhale slowly with an *ah!*

Close your eyes and sit back in your chairs with your feet firmly on the floor. As you begin to relax, take 3 deep breaths and exhale slowly with an AH!!!

Now sense, feel or imagine that you are sitting in a nice fluffy chair. This chair is attached to a long silver cord and starts lowering you into darkness. There is no fear here; and peace replaces curiosity. When the chair stops, you find yourself sitting in front of a golden door. You stand and reach out to touch the knob and the door opens slowly to reveal a grassy road ahead. It is a warm summer day with a gentle breeze blowing and you are barefoot and your toes welcome the freedom of the tickling grass.

You continue down this path and on either side of you there are your favorite flowers. Their fragrance is strong and subtle at the same time bringing a smile to your face and senses. If you choose you can pick some to take with you. As you stroll down the path, in the distance you see a lake with a small dock. This pleases you and you start to sprint toward it.

You can see sailboats floating along effortlessly. The colors of their sails are familiar. Red, orange, yellow, green, blue, indigo and violet. You decide to come and sit down on the end of the dock to get a better look at the boats. You place your flowers down beside you and of course curiously, put your hands in the water to test the temperature; now your toes. The water is warm and you smile as your inner child wants to join the experience. The sailboats seem to be enjoying your company too.

Now in your mine's eye; imagine that the boats represents the challenges in your life; so called burdens: pain, suffering, struggle, lack, guilt, shame and fear! Ask yourself, why do I continue to revisit these conflicts? If you choose to release these burdens or challenges, you may say this prayer aloud "I am now caused by God within me to release all _____". (fill in the blanks and take your time).

As you release, in time my beloved, all the boats; violet, indigo, blue, green, yellow, orange and red should drift away one by one.

This is God's wish for us all; *FREEDOM*!

Our time at the dock is coming to an end. The sun is starting to set surprisingly on a lake with no sail boats; just a gentle breeze!

Our spirits and souls are lifted in the name of *FREEDOM* in every way and on every level!

We leave the dock feeling refreshed and renewed; back down the grassy road to the golden door. It opens and there waits our fluffy chair to lift us up and out of the darkness; and back to this space and time.

When you are ready you may open your eyes.

Thank You!

New Moon

Today I would like to guide you on a little stay-cation (stay in your seats and go on a mental vacation). So sit back in your chairs; get comfortable and relax to get ready for some peaceful moments to be gentle with your self-care, self-love and self-celebration!

We will start with 3 OHMs to heighten the vibration in this space and invite the Holy Spirit to join us. (Immediately the room becomes full of LOVE energy! And we were ready to begin our journey).

See, feel or imagine that you are walking down a wooded path during a sweet spring evening. The sun is setting in the distance and you admire the beautiful colors that you see and embrace the warmth that you start to feel as you close your eyes and take in its magnificence. As you continue along this path; you come to a clearing with green grass smelling like the springtime you remember when you were younger and carefree.

In the distance you see a light from a fire that seems to be burning. You decide to walk toward it. As you get closer you see that it is a campfire; welcoming you to come and sit down and rest your body, mind and spirit. You feel at peace as you sit and watch the colors of the flames: red, orange, yellow, green, blue, indigo and violet.

Close your eyes and take in the colors as you meditate on what you want to manifest in your life now. Take your time and enjoy the warmth of the fire. It soothes your soul!

Suddenly you open your eyes and to your left there is a steep mountain. If you choose you may stay by the fire and reflect or you can choose to walk up the mountain.

You are not tired from this stroll; instead you feel energized as you reach the top. At the top you discover the New Moon waiting for your arrival! She is big, bright and white and seems to smile at you because She is glad that you chose the mountain path. Stand there for a moment and wish upon the stars that accompany this universal splendor designed just for your pleasure! Take it all in and know that you can revisit these images whenever you feel the need. Now you know it is time to return. As you turn to go back down the mountain; your spirit guide appears and offers you a gold gift box wrapped in a beautiful red bow. This gift is especially for you. When you open it, know that it is designed for your greatest and highest good!

As you reach the bottom of the mountain you notice that the campfire is going out and the colors violet, indigo, blue, green, yellow, orange and red are fading and you have just enough time to return down the wooded path. You are now uplifted and gifted by the Holy Spirit in every way and on every level. Take a moment to say" thank you GOD" for this stay-cation !!! When you are ready, open your eyes and return to this space!"

Your Higher Self

Get comfortable in your seats. Relax and if you choose on your own take 3 deeps breaths exhaling slowly with an AH!

Now sense, feel or imagine that you are standing in front of a white marble staircase. You decide to walk up this staircase and as you step slowly you feel pulsating energy under your feet and on the 1st step the color red; the 2nd is orange; the 3rd is yellow; the 4th is green; the 5th is blue; the 6th is indigo; on the last step is violet.

When you reach the top of the staircase; there is a silver door that suddenly opens to reveal a bright white light. This light surrounds you and it is warm and soothing. As you continue to walk, the light dissipates.

You find yourself walking down a grassy path with spring in the air. Your favorite flowers are blooming on either side of you and there are birds singing. You stop to take in this special gift from The Creator who is offering us the blessing of renewal and resurrection.

As you continue your stroll; you find yourself in front of a golden throne and to your surprise; this throne has a golden crown placed on the back of the seat. You walk up the 3 steps and decide to take your seat on your throne and place your crown on your head. You smile as you accept and receive the worthiness and deservingness energy that it represents.

When you do this; a band of Archangels appear dresses in the colors of the pulsating stairway that you used to get here. The Archangels surround you as they caress you with their wings in all the wounded places that need healing, including your chakras. Your root, sacral, solar plexus, heart. throat, third eye and crown.

You are relaxed with your eyes closed to receive this healing and transformation that you have called for. And if you choose; take your time and speak your desires aloud!

The Archangels are enjoying their time with you but it is time for them to leave you; you can sit still and absorb all the loving energy that you deserve to receive.

As you open your eyes you notice your spirit guide kneeling beside you and hands you a red velvet heart shaped box. You choose to open this box to find a gift for your greatest and highest good. See this gift and thank your guide who suddenly disappears. It is now time to return.

You stand tall as you prepare to leave your throne; with your crown worn majestically; and your gift, feeling regal and renewed (remember you can revisit this place at any time).

As you walk slowly back down the path to the white light; you feel refreshed and restored. The golden door opens to the marble stairs. You head is still held high as you step on to the still pulsating colors of the staircase. Violet, indigo, blue, green, yellow, orange and red. Remember this feeling as you prepare to return to this time and space!

When you are ready you may open your eyes!

Candles In The Mirror

Sit back, relax and put your feet firmly on the floor; uncross your hands and legs so as not to block the energy that you desire.

Take 3 deep breaths on your own, then together let us do 3 OHMs to raise the vibration in the room.

See, feel or imagine that you open a golden door to a room filled with lit white candles as well as candles of familiar colors; red, orange, yellow, green, blue, indigo and violet.

As you enter this room you see that there is a lovely sofa of your own design that summons your body, mind and spirit that deserves to sit and relax.

As you sit or lay on your customized sofa; you start to reflect on your life experiences. The good, the bad and the ugly. It is important to learn to love all of yourself unconditionally all of the time, always and always, and it is not an easy feat.

Close your eyes and imagine you as your best self at any part of your life's assignment. Take a moment to speak aloud anything that made you happy. Hold on to these feelings and embrace your unlimited deservingness.

When you open your eyes you notice that this room now has a mirror. You choose to get up and walk over to the mirror to admire your reflection which includes the candle lit room behind you.

This causes you to see yourself fully as you are now. You take the time to stare into this mirror and allow a true view of that magnificent you. Finally seeing yourself through new eyes of unconditional love as God sees you. Self-love is the key. Hold on to this feeling.

Now it is time to return; so take a last look at God's masterpiece that is you before leaving this sanctuary of peace and serenity.

As you pass the sofa thank it for its contribution to your restoration. You walk to return to the golden door and as you pass the colored candles you blow them out one by one. Violet, indigo, blue, green, yellow, orange and red. Only the white candles remain lit.

As you glance back to review the room and choose a big bright smile. You close the door gently behind you to return to your path and purpose knowing that you can always return to this space and time.

Keep this as a safe haven for your thoughts when darkness shows up in your life. Remember that unlimited deservingness is your birthright.

When you are ready open your eyes and return to this place and time.

Thank you.

Part III

Affirmations

Affirmations strengthen your spiritual muscle and set your intentions for personal growth and spiritual development. They are a symphony of syllables designed to activate your awareness, which may be thirst and needed to be watered with your willingness to know and believe. If you choose, you may declare out loud daily the affirmations that resonate with you. Repeat each one at least three times or until you feel the connection with your spirit.

I Know

1. I know that God loves me unconditionally, always.

2. I know I have faith in my faith.

3. I know abundance and prosperity are in my future.

4. I know God guides all things in my life for my greatest and highest good.

5. I know He is blessing me in every way and on every level.

Create Your Own "I Know" Affirmations

I Believe

1. I believe that God has unlimited blessings for me always.

2. I believe in gratitude for my gifts.

3. I believe that I am light in the universe.

4. I believe I can overcome all obstacles.

5. I believe in being open to accept and receive all the grace that God is giving me now.

Create Your Own "I Believe" Affirmations

I Am

1. I am accepting and allowing my destiny to unfold daily.
2. I am seeking the truth about my authenticity.
3. I am supporting my inner child's right to be reborn.
4. I am a cocoon of self-healing.
5. I am releasing all resistance to peace in my life.

Create Your Own "I Am" Affirmations

Prosperity Affirmations

(God is the Energy and Consciousness of Yes)

I am money in every infinite form.

I am freed from all grievances and blockages. I have totally forgiven myself.

I am the innocent child of God, and money flows to me freely.

I am caused by God right now to know, feel and believe that I always have more than enough money to share and to spare.

I am caused by God right now to know, feel and believe that I always have more than enough money to enjoy everything.

I am caused by God right now to know, feel and believe that I am deserving of love in the form of money.

Thank you, God! Thank you, God! Thank you, God!

Create Your Own Prosperity Affirmations
(You can create your own prosperity name—for example,
"Rhonda Wealthy Williams.")

Letter to Self-Forgiveness

Dear Self,

I want to apologize for some of my behavior the past few decades. Please forgive me for sabotaging our growth. I was unaware of the depth of self-loathing, denial and destructive lengths I would go to cripple our self-esteem. I was clueless and dismissive of the divine life God had for us, so I chose the hard-knock path for us! In spite of all the twists, turns, hills and valleys, I now stand grateful in our authentic truth.

Sincerely yours,
Rhonda

Create Your Own Letter of Self-Forgiveness

Letter to Forgiveness

Dear Forgiveness,

Thank you for continuing to support all of us in our journeys. Your gift just keeps on giving and allowing the growth to continue daily. Having compassion and love for ourselves and others can guide us to the newness of knowing that nothing is wasted and all is nurturing. I realize that gratitude is the driving force to spiritual freedom and self-love.

Lovingly yours,
Rhonda

Create Your Own Letter to Forgiveness

Create Your Own

Journal

Poems

Meditations

Glossary

Chakra
Energy points in the body*

Evolution
Changing the conscious and subconscious thinking

God References
You, Your, the Divine, Supreme, Him, Spirit, Creator

Grace
Mother God or Her

He-go
Male ego

Process
Stage of healing

Proetry
A fusion of prayer and poetry

Reiki
Ancient spiritual healing modality originating in Tibet

She-go
Female ego

The Enemy
Anything or anyone formed against you or your purpose
(including your own resistance)

*There are seven chakras: crown, third eye, throat, heart, solar plexus, sacral and root. The word is derived from the Sanskrit word for wheel or turning.

Recommended Reading

On Earth As It Is In Heaven:
A Path Of Liberation Received From The Holy
Spirit Of God And The Angels Of God
by Rev. Daniel Neusom

One Day My Soul Just Opened Up:
40 Days And 40 Nights Toward Spiritual
Strength And Personal Growth
by Iyanla Vanzant

Archangels 101:
How to Connect Closely with Archangels Michael, Raphael,
Gabriel, Uriel, and Others for Healing, Protection,
and Guidance
by Doreen Virtue

Empowering Women:
Every Woman's Guide to Successful Living
by Louise L. Hay

Psalms for Praying:
An Invitation to Wholeness
by Nan C. Merrill

www.ingramcontent.com/pod-product-compliance
Lightning Source LLC
LaVergne TN
LVHW040159080526
838202LV00042B/3232